First published 2007 by
A & C Black Publishers Ltd
38 Soho Square, London, W1D 3HB

www.acblack.com

ISBN 978-0-7136-7776-8 (hbk)
ISBN 978-0-7136-7769-0 (pbk)

A CIP catalogue for this book is available
from the British Library.

This book is produced using paper that is made from
wood grown in managed, sustainable forests. It is natural,
renewable and recyclable. The logging and manufacturing
processes conform to the environmental regulations
of the country of origin.

Printed and bound by MPG Books Ltd, Bodmin, Cornwall.

TOUGH JOBS
KNIGHT

Helen Greathead

Illustrated by Bob Dewar

A & C Black · London

Welcome to the Middle Ages

Imagine a time when:

• People didn't drive cars ... they rode horses.

• People didn't watch TV ... they had minstrels to sing, dance and tell stories.

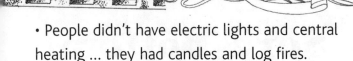

• People didn't have electric lights and central heating ... they had candles and log fires.

• People didn't wear jeans and carry mobile phones ... they wore armour and carried swords. Well, some of them did – the ones called knights.

The Middle Ages is the name for a time in history. It began when people started riding horses into battle and building castles to keep themselves safe. It ended when gunpowder was discovered and enemies found they could blast their way through those thick castle walls.

The Middle Ages started over 1000 years ago. It lasted more than 500 years.

A Sore Bottom

Let's pretend you live in the Middle Ages. Your house is modern and the biggest for miles around. It has paving slabs on the floors, carpets on the walls, and windows with real glass in them.

You even have some toy soldiers to play with. You are lucky. But your big brother is luckier. One day the house, the village and the land around it will be his, all his.

Today is your birthday. You are seven years old. Are you going to have a party? Will there be lots of presents? What about a cake? No, no and no again. Nobody celebrates birthdays in the Middle Ages. But there is a surprise for you...

Your dad pulls himself out of his comfy chair and hobbles out to the stables. He saddles up two horses. "Hop on," he says. "We're going for a ride."

The ride is a long one. It takes nearly all day. Hours of wobbling about in the saddle. Your bottom gets very sore and it can't be good for Dad's bad leg, either.

At long last, you come to a stop. "Hop off," says Dad. "We're here."

You are standing in front of an amazing castle. It's got brightly painted walls, battlements, a drawbridge, and a moat all around it.

"Phwoar, what's that smell?" you ask, peering down into the water.

"Careful," says Dad. "Don't fall in! There might be rusty spikes at the bottom to stab enemy soldiers."

You clatter across the drawbridge. Huge iron chains connect it to the castle walls. Your dad waves to the guards. They smile and wave back.

"What do they do?" you ask.

"The guards pull up the drawbridge if they spot enemies approaching," he says. "Then nobody can get into the castle!"

"Dad, look at that fantastic coat-of-arms!" you shout, pointing to the picture on the front of the gatehouse.

"That's Sir Cedric Blackswan's coat-of-arms," your dad says. "This is his castle."

You ride on through the gatehouse into a huge courtyard full of people rushing about. A teenage boy strides towards you.

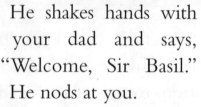

He shakes hands with your dad and says, "Welcome, Sir Basil." He nods at you.

"This is Squire William," says Dad. "He's going to be looking after you. Will is the castle's most promising squire, so listen to what he says, won't you?"

Squire William shakes your hand, "You can call me Will," he says, winking at you. "You're going to be our page. I'll train you in battle skills, but we'll both work for Sir Cedric. He can be quite fierce, but you'll soon get used to that."

You are confused. Why is Will telling you all this?

"Don't look so worried," Will laughs. "Training will be fun — and remember, you've got 14 years to get it right."

What! Now you understand. Dad's got you a job. It's what rich dads do with their younger sons. He is going to leave you at the castle for 14 years. That's how long it will take you to train to be … a knight!

Who's Who in the Middle Ages

The king is top dog...

Next come the lords and bishops...
Followed by the knights...

Last and least come the peasants.

The king owns all the land in the country, but he can give bits away

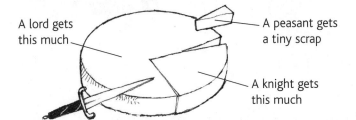

A lord gets this much

A peasant gets a tiny scrap

A knight gets this much

The king gets his land for free. But peasants and knights pay their lords, and then the lords pay the king.

And lords send their knights to fight for the king. But a peasant doesn't just pay the lord. He has to fight and work his master's land as well.

When a man dies, his oldest son gets everything.

The Dungeons

There's a lump in your throat as Dad rides off, but you know knights don't cry.

Will takes you into the main castle building. "This is the keep," he says. "It's where most of us eat and sleep. If there's an attack, women and children are sent in here. It's the safest place to be. Come on, want to have a look around?"

"Yes," you whisper. "But, er, Will, I'm busting for the um … you know…"

"You mean the garderobe!" Will snorts loudly. "Right, follow me."

He leads you to a staircase. You've never seen anything like it before. It has tiny steps that go round and round as you go up and up … and up and up.

Will shows you a little room at the top of the keep. You go inside and sit down. A whoosh of cold air hits your bottom. You slide off again and look down. The garderobe juts out from the castle wall. Far below is the murky water of the moat. Yuck, that's why it's so stinky.

When you've finished, you follow Will down another staircase and through a fancy wooden door. He puts a finger to his lips, "We shouldn't be here," he whispers.

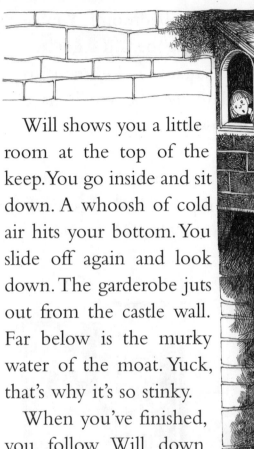

What a fabulous bedroom! You've never seen such a big bed. It's got fur pillowcases, and blankets and curtains to keep out the draft. Maybe you'll have a bed like this now you're going to be a knight.

"This room is the solar," says Will, forgetting to whisper. "And this door leads straight into the chapel."

Suddenly, an angry dressmaker rushes out from a wardrobe. "Out, out," she scolds. "What are you two doing in Sir Cedric's bedchamber?"

She chases you down another staircase. At the very bottom, you hear clatters and bangs, and angry shouts. Maybe it's the dungeon and somebody is being tortured? On the other hand, it smells quite nice.

"Welcome to the castle kitchen." says Will.

It must be five times the size of your kitchen at home! Right in the middle there's a great fire. A dead cow is roasting over it on a long pole. A boy about your age is turning a handle to keep the cow moving. There's sweat dripping off his nose.

"Supper's at sundown," says Will. "Not long to go."

"Is there time to see the dungeon?" you ask eagerly.

Will gives a wicked smile. "Come on then," he says, rushing across the courtyard into another tower.

Inside, it's damp and dingy. Will opens a grate in the floor. You kneel and peer in. Suddenly, he grabs your legs, and dangles you right down into the hole. "Aaargh!" you shout. The hole is deep, narrow and very, very dark.

"This is where we dump traitors," Will says, clasping your legs, tightly. "The prisoners are tied to a rope and lowered down to the bottom."

Your tummy rumbles loudly. "Food comes down on a rope, too," laughs Will.

The hole is horrible and cold. And if it flooded, you wouldn't just get wet in there. You'd drown.

Suddenly, Will pulls you out. You find yourself sprawled on the floor in front of a knight in shining armour. He's wearing the full kit: mail shirt, sword, shield, spurs and all. Wow, one day you might look like that! You don't know whether to kneel, bow, or stay where you are.

"S-sir Cedric," Will stammers. "Er, this is…"

"Why didn't you tell me Basil's boy was here?" Sir Cedric interrupts, helping you to your feet. "Welcome to my humble home!"

"Th-thank you, s-sir," you mumble.

"And what do you think you were doing to the poor lad, Will?" Sir Cedric demands.

Will looks at the ground.

"Any jokes being played, I want to be in on them, too!"

Your tummy rumbles again.

"Time for supper," Sir Cedric says. "Follow me."

Back inside the keep, you enter the Great Hall. It is sandwiched between the kitchens and the Solar. Everyone who lives and works in the castle is here. And they're all talking at once.

"Did Will tell you, we've got guests staying? So this will be your bedroom for tonight," shouts Sir Cedric. "Will gets a table, you can sleep on the floor."

You look down. The floor is covered with rushes. You spot old meat bones and bits of gristle. And, oh no, what's that…? Dog poo!

Sir Cedric
Gets Dressed

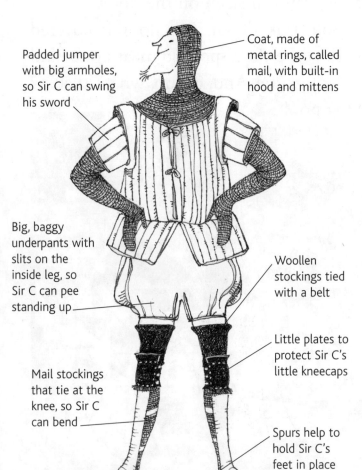

Padded jumper with big armholes, so Sir C can swing his sword

Coat, made of metal rings, called mail, with built-in hood and mittens

Big, baggy underpants with slits on the inside leg, so Sir C can pee standing up

Woollen stockings tied with a belt

Little plates to protect Sir C's little kneecaps

Mail stockings that tie at the knee, so Sir C can bend

Spurs help to hold Sir C's feet in place

Each piece of armour has to go on in the right order. The armour isn't as heavy as you'd think because the weight is spread out over Sir Cedric's body.

Sir C's crest, so people know who he is in battle

Helmet already has dents in, to make Sir C look scary!

Surcoat keeps Sir C's armour cool in the sun. The belt keeps the weight off his shoulders.

Broad sword, both edges are very sharp

Hard Work

After two weeks, the castle is starting to feel more like home. But so far, being a page isn't quite what you expected. It's fun training with Will, but he spends loads of time wrestling, swimming and fencing with the other squires.

You wish you were a squire – and you will be ... but not for seven years.

Most days, you have lessons in reading and writing with the castle priest. Today is different. You are stuck inside with a load of girls and the lady of the house. Posh girls from nearby are here to learn how to run a household.

The girls are teaching you to dance and making you listen to poetry. Knights are supposed to be good at these things, too. The girls aren't much older than you, but they are on the lookout for husbands already. Suddenly, they all seem to be smiling and gazing at you… Help!

"Let's go," booms a voice behind you.

It's Will. Phew, the girls were all staring at *him*.

"I've come to take the young 'un," says Will. "Sir Cedric's orders. He wants the lad to muck out the stables."

Huh, so much for training to be a knight! Most of the time you feel more like a servant.

The work is shattering, but just as you've nearly finished, Will pops back. "Fancy a ride?" he asks. Suddenly you don't feel tired at all. Of course you want a ride!

Will takes you over to Sir Cedric's horse, Goliath. He's the biggest horse you've ever seen. Sir Cedric calls Goliath his scariest weapon. Now you know why.

"He's a destrier," says Will. "A warhorse."

Will lifts you on and shoves a long pole in your hand. "This is a lance," he explains. "We use it in battle and in jousting competitions. You can throw it at your enemy, or stick it right into them."

Will points at a wooden target. "It's called a quintain," he says. "Hold the lance up, aim for the shield and charge as fast as you can."

You do as you're told. The lance is heavy and it wobbles all over the place. Still, you manage to hit the target.

"Yesss!" you shout and you try to punch the air. But before you know it, you're flat on your back on the ground and it hurts!

"You deserved that!" Will sniggers, helping you up. "Didn't they tell you, a good knight never boasts?"

No, they didn't. And they didn't warn you about the quintain either. Once you hit the target you have to move fast, or it will swing round and whack you with a heavy sack.

A Good Knight

Every page dreams of being a good knight one day. But that means being skilled in many different things. He has to:

• Learn to shoot a bow and arrow
• Work on his sword skills

• Build up his muscles

• Ride, ride and ride some more.

All these skills are really useful when it comes to fighting!

But a knight has to learn to be "chivalrous", too. That means:

- Being kind to children and ladies – especially rich ones

- Being true to God and the king
- Being modest (in other words, not boasting)
- Speaking properly and having good table manners
- Being nice to his enemies
- And even nicer to his horse.

SORRY!

DON'T MENTION IT

These skills help him to behave well at the castle – and to fight politely.

Enemy Attack

The next morning, Will wakes you by splashing cold, dirty water all over your face. "Mass in the chapel was cut short," he says, as he pushes you into the hallway.

It's freezing cold, but the castle is buzzing. What's going on?

You follow Will to the kitchens. The cooks are all hard at work, but the place smells disgusting. You sneak a look into the boiling pans. Some are bubbling with stinky, black stuff. They can't expect you to eat that?

"There's an enemy army approaching," Will explains at last. He picks up a pan of the black stuff and strides off with it.

Jack, the kitchen hand, struggles with another pan. You help him so you can ask what it is.

"Boiling tar," Jack explains. "We're taking it to the roof of the gatehouse. The guards can pour it through a hole in the ceiling straight onto enemy heads!"

At the gatehouse, you put the pan down. "The enemy soldiers won't get into the castle, will they?" you ask.

A guard answers. "They might have machines with them, and either try to bash the walls down or climb up them with ladders and belfry towers. But if they can't get in, they won't let us leave. They know we've got lots of people to feed. They might wait months and starve us out."

You wish you hadn't asked.

The drawbridge is up, and it looks like all the peasants in the land are inside the castle walls. Some are carrying nasty looking farm tools. Others have stuffed their shirts with straw.

Jack spots you staring at them. "The straw's the closest they'll get to armour. They can use the farm tools as weapons."

Knights in full armour and archers with their bows and arrows mingle with cows, pigs, horses and peasants. You can even see the lady of the house, ordering people about, snug in her fur-lined robe.

You spot Will dragging a mattress out of the keep and ask him what he's going to do with it. "It's to soften the blow of a battering ram," Will shouts. He signals

you to help him push it up the battlements. Sir Cedric is at the top, pulling it up. You rush up the ladder to join him.

"Will tells me you're doing well with the sword," says Sir Cedric, pushing an enormous broadsword into your hand. "Here, try this one. If a hand or head comes up over the wall, chop it off."

The sword handle is heavy, but the blade is light.

"If only Sir Basil could see you now," chuckles Sir Cedric, as you swish it about, just as Will taught you to …
and slash the mattress! Oops, feathers spill out everywhere.

"See how sharp it is!" laughs Sir Cedric.

How can he be laughing at a time like this?

Will climbs up to join you. "Shouldn't you be heading for the keep with all the other children?" he says. But he's brought you a helmet, so you know he's only joking.

Anyway, you don't want to miss out on the action. You've got to show Will and Sir Cedric what you're made of. You peer over the castle walls. It's a very long way down – and you can see the huge army getting closer. You grip the sword, bravely, ready for a real, live battle…

Under Siege

Cook makes up fire pots.

A mattress can soften the blow of a battering ram.

Archers fire from long, thin windows, called loopholes.

The enemy makes a bridge across the moat. Then they wheel the belfry tower up to the wall.

Knights and soldiers throw down boiling water, fire pots, stones and flaming arrows.

The enemy climbs up the back of the tower and a drawbridge helps them onto the battlements.

The enemy army build their war machines on the spot.

A huge catapult, called a trebuchet, throws boulders, dead animals, or even dead soldiers into the castle grounds.

The battering ram is for bashing down a castle wall.

When an army tries to attack a castle, it is called a siege. A siege can last for days, or months.

Hunting Party

Enemy soldiers are chanting and everyone else is shouting.

"Stop!" booms a voice and suddenly all is quiet.

Sir Cedric has climbed right to the top of the battlements. "Is that your coat-of-arms, Sir Marcus?" he shouts.

The enemy leader pulls of his helmet. "Sir Cedric!"

"Forget fighting," Sir Cedric shouts, "Let's feast instead!"

"What's going on?" you ask.

"Knights wear their crest in battle so everyone knows who's who. You don't want to kill your own people by mistake," Will explains. "Marcus's crest just saved our lives. He fought with Sir Cedric in France – they're old friends."

So that's that. Siege over. You can't help feeling relieved. Now everyone is busy thinking about something else … food. And if there's going to be a feast, first there must be a hunt!

Amazingly, you are allowed to join the hunting party.

"Next best thing to a fight," says Sir Cedric.

"Excellent training for battle," adds William.

"And not nearly so dangerous," you chip in, happily.

"Rubbish!" scoffs Will. "We're hunting wild boar. It might look like a hairy pig, but it's the fiercest animal in the forest."

Suddenly, the dogs are released from the kennels. Some of them are wearing armour.

"Watch out for stray spears and arrows," says Will.

Everyone heads off to the forest. Sir Cedric's huntsman is in front. He chooses a young boar and chases it towards the hunting party. The dogs yap wildly. You catch a glimpse of the boar's deadly tusks and gallop after it. It feels fantastic!

But the boar is difficult to catch. It darts this way and that. Everyone follows, twisting through the trees. When it is finally cornered, the boar is very angry.

Sir Cedric throws his spear and the boar falls to the ground. With a final blast of the horn, the hunt is over.

You haven't spent much time with Will. He's been off talking to everyone else. Suddenly, they all turn and look at you. Sir Cedric claps you on the back. "As youngest on the hunt," he says, seriously, "you have the honour of cutting up the kill."

He hands you a nasty looking dagger. Your heart stops, the dagger shakes in your hand. Then everyone starts laughing. You soon understand why. It's just another one of Will's stupid jokes.

Next day, the boar is cooked and the feast begins. You are at the top table with Sir Cedric and Sir Marcus. Are you sitting at Sir Cedric's side? Certainly not! You are a page. You must serve Sir Cedric's dinner.

There's a proper way to do everything. Each dish must be served in order and placed correctly on the table. You must hold the meat for Sir Cedric to carve – and remember which fingers to use.

Sir Cedric and Sir Marcus are talking. You pretend not to listen.

"We're off to war," says Sir Marcus. "And we need good knights to join us."

"Hmm," Sir Cedric answers. "You know, Will is an outstanding young squire..."

Most people have to share a cup. They must wipe their lips before they drink. Sir Cedric has a cup all to himself, but he still wipes his greasy lips on the tablecloth before drinking. He has excellent manners!

You serve the top table three whole courses of meat, birds, pies, jellies and

sugary puddings. Then it's your turn to eat – at the other end of the hall.

You share your plate with another page. The plate is made from bread, but you don't eat it. It soaks up the meat juices; then you chuck it under the table for the dog.

The banquet goes on for hours. At last, the sun goes down, but you don't have to go to bed. Tonight, you can stay up late to watch the minstrel. He can juggle, jump through hoops, dance and make up poems. At the end of his act, he tells a story about the greatest knight of all … King Arthur.

King Arthur, the Greatest Knight

There are loads of stories about King Arthur. In the Middle Ages, minstrels told the stories from memory. This was as close as the Middle Ages got to TV! The stories are full of magic:

• The young Arthur is the only one who can pull a magical sword from a stone. This proves that he is the true king of Britain.
• Arthur's best friend, Lancelot, is brought up by a fairy.

• Arthur's advisor is a wizard, called Merlin.

Nobody knows who Arthur really was:

• Some people think there wasn't just one Arthur, but there were lots of them! His stories really tell us the deeds of many honest, brave knights. They are examples for all knights to follow.

• Other people think there was only one Arthur, and he didn't really die. Instead, he is sleeping in a cave somewhere in Wales. One day, when his country really needs him, he'll come back and fight again.

Sir Will

A few days later, there is big news. Will is to be knighted, even though he's just 17.

"I've only once seen a squire as talented as Will," Sir Marcus says. "We need a man like him to fight with us."

So Will is off to battle! The knighting ceremony is tomorrow.

You get to stay up all night to help Will, but it's really boring. You wait outside the castle chapel, while Will confesses his sins. It takes ages. You're not surprised – he must be remembering all the nasty tricks he's played on you.

Then, Will has a bath in rose water to help wash away his sins. But you've heard a bath can wash away your strength, too.

Next morning, you help Will with his outfit. He wears a sort of long, white dress. It's a bit girly, but you don't say that to Will.

In the chapel, the ceremony is beginning. The priest talks a lot about being honest and true in battle and at home.

Out in the courtyard, you help buckle Sir Cedric's armour onto Will piece by piece. As Will is the youngest son of seven, he can't afford his own armour.

Will kneels and his lordship says, "I dub thee knight. Be brave, ready and loyal." Then he whacks Will so hard on the 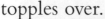shoulder with his sword, Will nearly topples over.

The serious bit is over. Hurray! It's time for the joust. Young knights from far and wide have come to test Will's skill.

Across the field you spot your dad! You wave and jump up and down, but he doesn't notice you. It seems everyone else wants to talk to him, too.

The herald sounds his trumpet. The joust is about to start! You sneak into her ladyship's tent and watch with the girls. One of them keeps sighing and pretending to faint. She can't take her eyes off Will. She's tied her hankie around his arm. This is called a favour – it means Will is entering the joust for her!

Will rides Goliath onto the field. They are wearing matching robes. Goliath has armour on, too.

The first knight lines up against Will, a trumpet blares and the joust begins. The two knights charge towards each other. Almost at once, the stranger knocks Will hard with his lance. The lances are blunt, but a blow still hurts. You worry that the bath has taken Will's strength away after all.

Luckily, Will soon gets into his stride. As the knights charge forward again, he knocks the challenger off his horse. Then he climbs down to finish the fight on foot.

Will wins! In fact, he beats one knight after another and wins every round. You can see why they made him a knight. Will really is brilliant! By the end of the contest he has won himself horses and a choice of armour and weapons.

Everyone is talking about Will. That girl is following him around, looking all dreamy. Your dad shakes him by the hand, but you can't get near either of them. If only you could be brilliant, like Will. Then your dad would notice you.

"He's just like Sir B in his younger days, before he wounded his leg," says Sir Cedric.

Sir Marcus laughs. "Remember when Sir B had his helmet knocked back-to-front – and still went on to win the joust?"

"He was unbeatable on the battlefield, too," smiles Sir Cedric. "He once captured 100 enemy knights in a day. He got rich on the money they paid him to free them."

You wonder who this Sir B is. He sounds amazing! Suddenly, an arm grabs you round the waist and you find yourself flying into the air, and onto your dad's shoulders.

Sir Cedric and Sir Marcus rush towards you.

"Sir B!" they cry. "Reckon Will's as good as you used to be?"

What! Your dad is Sir B? Sir B is your dad? *He's* the one who did all those daring deeds? Never!

"Every bit as good," your dad says, as Will comes over. "You did well, Will. But watch out! One day this little knight is going to be better than both of us."

That's right, you decide. One day you're going to be the best, most famous knight ever. Getting there is going to be a tough job, but you think you can do it.

Famous Knights – Three of the Best

There were no newspapers or magazines in the Middle Ages, so the best way to get famous was on the battlefield or at a tournament. The most famous knights had some surprising stories.

William Marshall was famous because:

- He was nearly hanged by the king when he was five (the king was really after William's dad)
- He was absolutely brilliant at jousting and earned himself a fortune
- He married the wealthiest woman in England
- He paid for a book to be written about himself (so he would carry on being famous long after he was dead).

Joan of Arc was famous because:
- She was a girl knight
- She was a peasant, not a noble
- She carried a banner instead of a sword
- She was great at working out how to win battles
- She never ever killed anybody
- She was burned to death by the English when she was just 19.

The Black Prince was famous because:
- He was heir to the throne of England
- He commanded and won a battle at just 16
- He won loads more battles
- He wore black armour
- He was very polite at banquets
- He was very nasty in battle
- He never got to be king, because he died before his dad.

Glossary

battlements – the top of the castle walls

bishop – a leader of the church

broadsword – a sword with a wide blade and two sharp edges

chivalrous – polite and honourable

coat-of-arms – the symbols on a knight's shield or surcoat, which show the army he belongs to

drawbridge – a gate that lowers across a moat

dub – to make a squire a knight by touching them on the shoulder with a sword

dungeon – a place where prisoners were kept

favour – a gift given by a lady to a knight so that he will fight the joust for her

garderobe – the castle toilet

gatehouse – the entrance to the castle

great hall – the room where everyone in the castle ate their meals

gunpowder – an explosive powder used to fire guns and canon

heir – someone who will inherit money, land or a title when their father dies

herald – a messenger; someone who brings news

joust – a competition between two knights, with weapons, on horseback

keep – the main castle tower

lance – a long weapon used on horseback

lord – the owner of a castle and its land

minstrel – an entertainer

moat – a water-filled ditch around a castle

mail – armour made from knitted metal rings

noble – someone with a title, e.g. lord or lady

page – the first stage of training to be a knight

peasant – someone who works on the land

quintain – a target used to practise lance skills

sir – the title used for a knight

squire – the second stage in a knight's training

solar – the main castle bedroom

spurs – the metal spikes worn on the back of a knight's heel, used to keep his horse moving

surcoat – a loose tunic worn over armour

siege – an attack on a castle by an enemy army

tar – a sticky, black liquid used to protect wood

tournament – a sporting contest in which knights jousted for a prize

visor – part of the helmet that can be pulled down to cover the face

63

WITH SO MANY **TOUGH JOBS** TO CHOOSE FROM...

WHICH ONE WILL **YOU** TRY NEXT?